GOLF IT'S A FUNNY OLD GAME

THE FUNNIEST QUOTES ABOUT GOLF

M PREFONTAINE

I

CONTENTS

Introduction

For us rabbits the game of golf is a constant battle between fantasy and reality. The great hopes and ambitions that accompany us on the first tee quickly evaporate by a combination of mother nature, gravity and the cruelest of luck.

One of the charms of the Great Game is that we are constantly chasing what is, in theory, attainable but in reality highly elusive. It is a perpetual series of occasions for hope.

David Feherty summed it up when he said;
Golf can best be defined as an endless series of tragedies obscured by the occasional miracle.

It is astonishing how long the occasional miracle can remain in the memory to the total eclipse of all else. Golf is a game whose hook is baited with hope.

This book is a compendium of quotes from players who have been similarly troubled by the journey from great hopes to cruel reality.

I hope you enjoy their reflections.

As it Lies

I have a tip that can take five strokes off anyone's golf game: it's called an eraser.
Arnold Palmer

The statute of limitations on forgotten strokes is two holes.
Leslie Nielsen

Counting on your opponent to inform you when he breaks a rule is like expecting him to make fun of his own haircut.
Anon

The number of shots taken by an opponent who is out of sight is equal to the square root of the sum of the number of curses heard plus the number of swishes.
Michael Green

Golf is a lot of walking, broken up by disappointment and bad arithmetic.
Earl Wilson

Golf is a game in which you yell "fore," shoot six, and write down five.
Paul Harvey

The best wood in most amateurs' bags is the pencil.
Chi Chi Rodriguez

A "gimme" can best be defined as an agreement between two golfers, neither of whom can putt very well.

Anon

Golf is a game in which the ball lies poorly and the players well.

Art Rosenbaum

Isn't it fun to go out on the course and lie in the sun?

Bob Hope

The difference between golf and government is that in golf you can't improve your lie.

George Deukmejian

My golf score seems to improve considerably when I have the score card.

Anon

The only sure rule in golf is he who has the fastest cart never has to play the bad lie.

Mickey Mantle

I don't exaggerate - I just remember big.

Chi Chi Rodriguez

Golf appeals to the idiot in us and the child. Just how childlike golf players become is proven by their frequent inability to count past five.

John Updike

You are meant to play the ball as it lies, a fact that may help to touch on your own objective approach to life.
Grantland Rice

To some golfers, the greatest handicap is the ability to add correctly.
Anon

The income tax has made more liars out of the American people than golf has.
Will Rogers

Golf... is the infallible test. The man who can go into a patch of rough alone, with the knowledge that only God is watching him, and play his ball where it lies, is the man who will serve you faithfully and well.
P.G. Wodehouse

Most people play a fair game of golf - if you watch them.
Joey Adams

A stroke does not occur unless it is observed by another golfer.
Anon

An extra ball in the pocket is worth two strokes in the bush.
Anon

You might as well praise a man for not robbing a bank as to praise him for playing by the rules.
Bobby Jones

I used to play golf with a man who cheated so badly that he once had a hole in one and wrote a zero on his scorecard.
Ronnie Corbett

Golf is the hardest game in the world to play, and the easiest to cheat at.
Dave Hill

On a recent survey, 80% of golfers admitted cheating. The other 20% lied.
Bruce Lansky

The greatest liar in the world is the golfer how claims he plays the game for merely exercise.
Tommy Bolt

The main problem with keeping your eye on the ball is that you have to take it off your opponent.
Bruce Lansky

Golf has more rules than any other game because golf has more cheaters than any other game.
Bruce Lansky

If your opponent has trouble remembering whether he shot a six or a seven, he probably shot an eight (or worse).
Anon

CLOTHES

Hockey is a sport for white men. Basketball is a sport for black men. Golf is a sport for white men dressed like black pimps.
Tiger Woods

"Play it as it lies" is one of the fundamental dictates of golf. The other is "Wear it if it clashes."
Henry Beard

Although golf was originally restricted to wealthy, overweight Protestants, today it's open to anybody who owns hideous clothing.
Dave Barry

The last thing you want to do is shoot 80 wearing 'tartan troosers'.
Ian Poulter

The reason most people play golf is to wear clothes they would not be caught dead in otherwise.
Roger Simon

I'd give up golf if I didn't have so many sweaters.
Bob Hope

I think I've heard somebody say that I was a well-dressed golfer. I guess that has something to do with the fact that a lot of people who play golf don't dress very well.
Arnold Palmer

Doug Sanders' outfit has been described as looking like the aftermath of a direct hit on a pizza factory.
Dave Marr

The only thing that scares me is the Americans' dress sense.
Mark James

Golf is not a sport. Golf is men in ugly pants, walking.
Rosie O'Donnell

No golfer ever swung too slow. No golfer ever played too fast. No golfer ever dressed too plainly.
Henry Beard

When Bill Clinton played golf... he wore jogging shoes, and his shirt was hanging out over painter's pants. Golf needs Clinton like it needs a case of ringworm.
Rick Reilly

To play golf you need goofy pants and a fat ass.
Happy Gilmore

You can't call it a sport. You don't run, jump, you don't shoot, you don't pass. All you have to do is buy some clothes that don't match.
Steve Sax

I'd give up golf if I didn't have so many sweaters.
Bob Hope

PUTTING

I learned one thing from jumping motorcycles that was of great value on the golf course, the putting green especially: Whatever you do, don't come up short.
Evel Knievel

These greens are so fast I have to hold my putter over the ball and hit it with the shadow.
Sam Snead

If you drink, don't drive. Don't even putt.
Dean Martin

The least thing upset him on the links. He missed short putts because of the uproar of butterflies in the adjoining meadows.
P.G. Wodehouse

It's so bad I could putt off a tabletop and still leave the ball halfway down the leg.
J.C. Snead

When I putt, my emotions collide like tectonic plates. It's left my memory circuits full of scars that won't heal.
Mac O'Grady

Half of golf is fun; the other half is putting.
Peter Dobereiner

Missing a short putt does not mean you have to hit your next drive out of bounds.
Henry Cotton

A good player who is a great putter is a match for any golfer. A great hitter who cannot putt is a match for no one.
Ben Sayers

The devoted golfer is an anguished soul who has learned a lot about putting, just as an avalanche victim has learned a lot about snow.
Dan Jenkins

Putts get real difficult the day they hand out the money.
Lee Trevino

Putting allows the touchy golfer two to four opportunities to blow a gasket in the short space of two to forty feet.
Tommy Bolt

Bets lengthen putts and shorten drives.
Henry Beard

The divorce is from my old putter. I think it's final - at least we're due for a long separation. I've suffered with that old putter for two years now. It got so rude I couldn't stand it.
Shelly Hamlin

Even when times were good, I realized that my earning power as a golf professional depended on too many ifs and putts.
Gene Sarazen

Ninety percent of putts that are short, don't go in.
Yogi Berra

I was lying ten and had a thirty-five-foot putt. I whispered over my shoulder: "How does this one break?" And my caddie said, "Who cares?"
Jack Lemmon

I made the last putt. It just didn't go in.
Tom Kite

A tap-in is a putt that is short enough to be missed one-handed.
Henry Beard

Why am I using a new putter? Because the last one didn't float too well.
Craig Stadler

Putt in haste and repent at leisure
Gerald Batchelor

No putt ever got longer as the result of being marked.
Leslie Nielsen

Bad putting is due more to the effect the green has upon the player than it has upon the action of the ball.
Bobby Jones

That green appears smaller than a pygmy's nipple.
David Feherty

The easiest shot in golf is the fourth putt.
Rex Lardner

A coarse golfer is one who has to shout 'fore' when he putts.
Michael Green

If you can imagine a hole halfway down the bonnet of a Volkswagen Beetle – and then you have to putt it from the roof.
Nick Faldo

I'd rather watch a cabbage grow than a man worrying his guts over a two-foot putt.
Michael Parkinson

That putt had more breaks than a government job.
Brian Weis

Mary had a little putt,
she needed it for par.
Mary has a second putt,
the first one went too far.
Margaret Kennard

In my house in Houston I still have that putter with which I missed that two-and-a-half-foot putt to win the Open. It's in two pieces.
Doug Sanders

There is no similarity between golf and putting; they are two different games, one played in the air, and the other on the ground.
Ben Hogan

Bumpy greens don't bother me anymore. Since I've become an analyst, I don't see the problem.

David Feherty

ETIQUETTE

The first chapter in the Rules of Golf is etiquette.
Apparently, everyone starts reading at chapter two.
 Nick Mokelke

One almost expects one of the players to peer into the
monitor and politely request viewers to refrain from
munching so loudly on cheese and crackers while the
golfers are trying to reach the greens.
Pete Alfano

Go ahead and putt, you are not interrupting my
conversation.
Robert E. Zorn

Talking to a golf ball won't do you any good, unless you
do it while your opponent is teeing off.
Bruce Lansky

Golf is the only game in which a precise knowledge of the
rules can earn one a reputation for bad sportsmanship.
Patrick Campbell

If you think it's hard to meet new people, try picking up
the wrong golf ball.
Jack Lemmon

If your adversary is badly bunkered there's no rule
against your standing over him and counting his strokes
aloud with increasing gusto as their number mounts up
Horace Hutchinson

Not every golfer can take strokes off his own score, but with the proper techniques you can help your opponent gain strokes on his score.
Leslie Nielsen

There are three things in the world that he held in the smallest esteem - slugs, poets and caddies with hiccups.
P.G. Wodehouse

Show me a man who is a good loser and I'll show you a man who is playing golf with his boss.
James Patrick Murray

According to the Captain of The Honorable Company of Edinburgh Golfers, striking your opponent or caddie at St Andrews, Hoylake or Westward Ho! meant that you lost the hole, except on medal days when it counted as a rub of the green.
Herbert Warren Wind

If a ball comes to rest in dangerous proximity to a hippopotamus or crocodile, another ball may be dropped at a safe distance, no nearer the hole, without penalty.
Local rule at Nyanza GC, Uganda

Few pleasures on earth match the feeling that comes from making a loud bodily function noise just as a guy is about to putt.
Dave Barry

The interesting thing about a coarse golfers' language is that to listen to him one would think his bad shots came as a surprise.

Michael Green

Golfers are dull robots carrying sticks. They don't even spit or scratch their privates like other athletes.

Lewis Grizzard

What is the penalty for killing a photographer – one stroke or two?

Davis Love III

Everyone replaces his divot after a perfect approach shot.

Anon

THE GREAT GAME

Golf. You hit down to make the ball go up. You swing left and the ball goes right. The lowest score wins. And on top of that, the winner buys the drinks.
Anon

Golf is a good walk spoiled.
Mark Twain

In golf, humiliations are the essence of the game.
Alastair Cooke

A Major golf tournament is 40,000 sadists watching 144 masochists.
Thomas Boswe

The game of golf is an enigma wrapped in a mystery impaled on a conundrum.
Peter Alliss

Golf is an exercise in Scottish pointlessness for people who are no longer able to throw telephone poles at each other.
Florence King

While playing golf today I hit two good balls. I stepped on a rake.
Henry Youngman

Golf can best be defined as an endless series of tragedies obscured by the occasional miracle.
David Feherty

Golf is 20 percent mechanics and technique. The other 80 percent is philosophy, humor, tragedy, romance, melodrama, companionship, camaraderie, cussedness and conversation.
Grantland Rice

Professional golf is the only sport where, if you win 20 percent of the time, you're the best.
Jack Nicklaus

In no other sport must the spectator move.
John Updike

Golf is so popular simply because it is the best game in the world at which to be bad.
A.A. Milne

It is more satisfying to be a bad player at golf. The worse you play, the better you remember the occasional good shot.
Nubar Gulbenkian

Golf is like a love affair. If you don't take it seriously, it's no fun; if you do take it seriously, it breaks your heart.
Arthur Daley

Golf is a game that is played on a five-inch course — the distance between your ears.
Bobby Jones

Golf is the cruelest of sports. Like life, it's unfair. It's a harlot. A trollop. It leads you on. It never lives up to its promises.... It's a boulevard of broken dreams. It plays with men. And runs off with the butcher.
Jim Murray

Golf is a fascinating game. It has taken me nearly forty years to discover that I can't play it.
Ted Ray

The people who gave us golf and called it a game are the same people who gave us bag pipes and called it music.
Anon

Golf is a day spent in a round of strenuous idleness.
William Wordsworth

I regard golf as an expensive way of playing marbles.
G.K. Chesterton

I think golf is a waste of time and a waste of a sunny afternoon. I also stink at it. I have never found anything, including divorce and a sexual harassment suit, more frustrating.
Jay Mohr

A passion, an obsession, a romance, a nice acquaintanceship with trees, sand, and water.
Bob Ryan

There is one thing in this world that is dumber than playing golf. That is watching someone else playing golf. What do you actually get to see? Thirty-seven guys in polyester slacks squinting at the sun. Doesn't that set your blood racing?
Peter Andrews

If I'm on the course and lightning starts, I get inside fast. If God wants to play through, let him.
Bob Hope

Golf is the most fun you can have without taking your clothes off.
Chi Chi Rodriguez

Golf is not, on the whole, a game for realists. By its exactitudes of measurements it invites the attention of perfectionists.
Heywood Hale Broun

Golf seems to me an arduous way to go for a walk. I prefer to take the dogs out.
Princess Anne

That ball is so far left, Lassie couldn't find it if it was wrapped in bacon.
David Feherty

An interesting thing about Golf is that no matter how badly you play, it is always possible to get worse.
Anon

I play in the low 80s. If it's any hotter than that, I won't play.
Joe E. Lewis

Fifty years ago, 100 white men chasing one black man across a field was called the Ku Klux Klan. Today it's called the PGA Tour.
Alex Hay

Golf without mistakes is like watching haircuts. A dinner without wine.
Jim Murray

If I hit it right, it's a slice. If I hit it left, it's a hook. If I hit it straight, it's a miracle.
Anon

It took me seventeen years to get three thousand hits in baseball. I did it in one afternoon on the golf course.
Hank Aaron

Golf's three ugliest words: still your shot.
Dave Marr

The game lends itself to fantasies about our abilities.
Peter Alliss

Golf is a game of expletives not deleted.
Dr Irving A. Gladstone

Golf is deceptively simple and endlessly complicated.
Arnold Palmer

Golf is like life in a lot of ways - All the biggest wounds are self-inflicted.
Bill Clinton

Golf is a game to be played between cricket and death.
Colin Ingleby-Mackenzie

I'm not feeling very well - I need a doctor immediately. Ring the nearest golf course.
Groucho Marx

It's a funny old game. One day you're a statue, the next you're a pigeon.
Peter Alliss

Golf is the Esperanto of sport. All over the world golfers talk the same language - much of it nonsense and much unprintable - endure the same frustrations, discover the same infallible secrets of putting, share the same illusory joys.
Henry Longhurst

I could never believe in a game where the one who hits the ball the least wins.
Winston Churchill

By the time a man can afford to lose a golf ball he can't hit it that far.
Lewis Grizzard

Golf is an ideal diversion, but a ruinous disease.
Bertie Forbes

I had played so poorly recently, I started thinking that maybe I should do something else. Then I saw my friends going to work every day and realized that my life wasn't so bad.
Steve Pate

Golf is very much like a love affair, if you don't take it seriously, it's no fun, if you do, it breaks your heart. Don't break your heart, but flirt with the possibility.
Louise Suggs

Playing the game I have learned the meaning of humility. It has given me an understanding of futility of the human effort.
Abba Eban

If you really want to get better at golf, go back and take it up at a much earlier age.
Thomas Mulligan

No game designed to be played with the aid of personal servants by right handed men who can't even bring along their dogs can be entirely good for the soul.
Bruce McCall

RELIGION

The only time my prayers are never answered is on the golf course.
Billy Graham

It's easy to see golf not as a game at all but as some whey-faced, nineteenth-century Presbyterian minister's fever dream of exorcism achieved through ritual and self-mortification.
Bruce McCall

Golf gives you an insight into human nature, your own as well as your opponent's.
Grantland Rice

I just hope I don't have to explain all the times I've used His name in vain when I get up there.
Bob Hope

Some of us worship in churches, some in synagogues, some on golf courses.
Adlai Stevenson

There are two things you can do with your head down — play golf and pray.
Lee Trevino

I never pray to God to make a putt. I pray to God to help me react good if I miss a putt.
Chi Chi Rodriguez

If you call on God to improve the results of a shot while it is still in motion, you are using "an outside agency" and subject to appropriate penalties under the rules of golf.
Henry Longhurst

Golf is like faith: it is the substance of things hoped for, the evidence of things not seen.
Arnold Haultain

Statisticians estimate that crime among good golfers is lower than in any class of the community except possibly bishops.
P. G. Wodehouse

Always keep in mind that if God didn't want a man to have mulligans, golf balls wouldn't come three to a sleeve.
Dan Jenkins

If God had intended a round to take more than three hours he would not have invented Sunday lunch.
Jimmy Hill

I'm gambling that when we get into the next life, Saint Peter will look at us and ask, "Golfer?" And when we nod, he will step aside and say, "Go right in; you've suffered enough." One warning, if you do go in and the first thing you see is a par 3 surrounded by water, it ain't heaven.
Jim Murray

I try to work with God as a partner.
Gary Player

Golf may be played on Sunday, not being a game within the view of the law, but being a form of moral effort.
Stephen Leacock

One golfer a year is hit by lightning. This may be the only evidence we have of God's existence.
Steve Ayle

Prayer never works for me on the golf course. That may have something to do with my being a terrible putter.
Rev. Billy Graham

If God wanted you to putt cross-handed, he would have made your left arm longer.
Lee Trevino

The Player

In the Bob Hope Golf Classic the participation of
President Gerald Ford was more than enough to remind
you that the nuclear button was at one stage at the
disposal of a man who might have either pressed it by
mistake or else pressed it deliberately in order to obtain
room service.
Clive James

Corey Pavin is the only golfer whose practice swing is
worse than his actual swing.
Johnny Miller

Hubert Green swings like a drunk trying to find a keyhole
in the dark.
Jim Murray

Whenever I play with him (President Ford), I usually try
to make it a foursome - the President, myself, a
paramedic and a faith healer.
Bob Hope

If Jack Nicklaus had to play my tee shots, he couldn't
break 80. He'd be a pharmacist with a string of
drugstores in Ohio.
Lee Trevino

Lee Trevino is the only man I know who talks on his
backswing.
Charley McClendon

The only time Nick Faldo opens his mouth is to change feet.
David Feherty

Shortly after I started playing golf with Jerry Ford I thought it was time to take some lessons. Not golf lessons. First aid.
Bob Hope

Golf, like the measles, should be caught young, for, if postponed to riper years, the results may be serious.
P.G. Wodehouse

I wouldn't bet anyone against Byron Nelson. The only time he left the fairway was to pee in the bushes.
Jackie Burke

(Arnold Palmer) told me how I could cut eight strokes off my score - skip one of the par 3s.
Bob Hope

Watching Sam Snead practice hitting golf balls is like watching a fish practice swimming.
John Schlee

When Nicklaus plays wells well, he wins. When he plays badly, he finishes second. When he plays terribly, he finishes third.
Johnny Miller

Bob Hope has a beautiful short game. Unfortunately, it's off the tee.
Jimmy Demaret

If conversation was fertilizer, Trevino would be up to his neck in grass all the time.
Fuzzy Zoeller

Arnie has more people watching him park the car than we do out on the course.
Lee Trevino

His golf bag does not contain a full set of irons.
Robin Williams

Gerald Ford (is) the most dangerous driver since Ben-Hur.
Bob Hope

It's not hard to find Gerald Ford on a golf course - just follow the wounded.
Bob Hope

I owe everything to golf. Where else could a guy with an IQ like mine make this much money.
Hubert Green

Worst haircut I've ever seen in my life. And I've had a few bad ones. It looks like he (John Daly) has a divot over each ear.
David Feherty

I do not let a bad score ruin my enjoyment for golf.
Darrell Royal

Never leave your opponent with the sole responsibility for thinking of all the things that might go wrong with his shot.

Anon

Show me a man with a great golf game, and I'll show you a man who has been neglecting something.

John F. Kennedy

I wish I could play my normal golf game.... just once.

Anon

A good golf partner is one who's always slightly worse than you.

Anon

When I die, bury me on the golf course so my husband will visit.
Anon

Give me the fresh air, a beautiful partner, and a nice round of golf, and you can keep the fresh air and the round of golf.
Jack Benny

"After all, golf is only a game," said Millicent. Women say these things without thinking. It does not mean that there is a kink in their character. They simply don't realise what they are saying.
P.G. Wodehouse

I am sorry Nick Faldo couldn't be here this week. He is attending the birth of his next wife.
David Feherty

Golf and sex are the only things you can enjoy without being good at them.
Jimmy DeMaret

I understand why marriages break up over golf. I can't even talk about my own handicap because it's too upsetting.
Shia LeBeouf

Golf is like marriage, If you take yourself too seriously it won't work, and both are expensive.
Anon

I don't have a life, I really don't. I'm as close to a nun as you can be without the little hat. I'm a golf nun.
Gabrielle Reece

Someone once told me that there is more to life than golf. I think it was my ex-wife.
Bruce Lansky

A good one iron shot is about as easy to come by as an understanding wife.
Dan Jenkins

Golf is played by 20 million mature American men whose wives think they are out having fun.
Jim Bishop

A golf course is the epitome of all that is purely transitory in the universe; a space not to dwell in, but to get over as quickly as possible.
Jean Giraudoux

You can make a lot of money in this game. Just ask my ex-wives. Both of them are so rich that neither of their husbands work.
Lee Trevino

All my exes wear Rolexes.
John Daly

My wife doesn't care what I do when I'm away. As long as I don't enjoy myself.
Lee Trevino

Playing golf is like raising children. You keep thinking you'll do better next time.
E.C. McKenzie

Golf is a marriage. If I had to choose between my wife and my putter, well, I would miss her.
Gary Player

I asked my wife if she wanted a Versace dress, diamonds or pearls as a present and she said, 'No!'. When I asked her what she did want, she said a divorce, but I told her I wasn't intending to spend that much.
Nick Faldo (After he had won the Million Dollar Challenge in South Africa)

The average golfer's handicap is his IQ. Girls, believe me, if your hubby keeps golfing, he will soon have the brain frequency of a lower primate.
Kathy Lette

Nobody in pro golf reads the money list better than ex-wives.
Dan Jenkins

When you retire, your wife gets twice as much husband and half as much money. I have to keep playing.
Chi Chi Rodriguez

I am tired of all these golfers who are happy with second place. The only one who will like you if you come in second place is your wife and your dog. And that is only if you have a good wife and a good dog.
Gary Player

There are three roads to ruin; women, gambling, and golf. The most pleasant is with women, the quickest is with gambling, but the surest is with golf.
Andrew Perry

I owe a lot to my parents, especially my mother and father.
Greg Norman

It's amazing how a golfer who never helps out around the house will replace his divots, repair his ball marks, and rake his sand traps.
Anon

On the Course

Happiness is a long walk with a putter.
Greg Norman

If there is a ball on the fringe and a ball in the bunker, your ball is in the bunker. If both balls are in the bunker, yours is in the footprint.
Anon

I know I am getting better at golf because I am hitting fewer spectators.
Gerald R. Ford

Golf is a game whose aim is to hit a very small ball into an ever-smaller hole, with weapons singularly ill-designed for the purpose.
Winston S. Churchill

How did I make a twelve on a par five hole? It's simple - I missed a four-foot putt for an eleven.
Arnold Palmer

What goes up must come down. But don't expect it to come down where you can find it.
Lily Tomlin

The woods are full of long drivers.
Harvey Penick

When your shot has to carry over a water hazard, you can either hit one more club or two more balls.
Henry Beard

Hazards attract; fairways repel.
Anon

The secret of golf is to turn three shots into two.
Bobby Jones

Hitting the ball is the fun part of it, but the fewer times you hit the ball the more fun you have.
Lou Graham

Too much ambition is a bad thing to have in a bunker.
Bobby Jones

If your adversary is badly bunkered, there is no rule against your standing over him and counting his strokes aloud, with increasing gusto as their number mounts up; but it will be a wise precaution to arm yourself with the niblick before doing so, so as to meet him on equal terms.
Horace Hutchinson

The real success in golf lies in turning three shots into two.
Bobby Locke

It's often necessary to hit a second shot to really appreciate the first one.
Henry Beard

Drive for show, putt for dough, shank for comic relief.
Anon

The difference between a sand trap and water hazard is the difference between a car crash and an airplane crash. You have a chance of recovering from a car crash.
Bobby Jones

A ball will always come to rest halfway down a hill, unless there is sand or water at the bottom.
Henry Beard

My golf is improving. Yesterday I hit the ball in one.
Jane Swan

Golf is not a game of great shots. It's a game of most accurate misses. The people who win make the smallest mistakes.
Gene Littler

Real golfers have 2 handicaps: one for bragging and one for betting.
Anon

I had a wonderful experience on the golf course today. I had a hole in nothing. Missed the ball and sank the divot.
Don Adams

My favorite shots are the practice swing and the conceded putt. The rest can never be mastered.
Lord Robertson

I'll always remember the day I broke ninety. I had a few beers in the clubhouse and was so excited I forgot to play the back nine.
Bruce Lansky

I'd like to see the fairways more narrow. Then everybody would have to play from the rough, not just me.
Seve Ballesteros

I would like to deny all allegations by Bob Hope that during my last game of golf, I hit an eagle, a birdie, an elk and a moose.
Gerald Ford

I wish I was playing in the [1985] Ryder Cup team. How could they beat me? I've been struck by lightning, had two back operations, and been divorced twice.
Lee Trevino

I played so bad, I got a get-well card from the IRS.
Johnny Miller

Playing polo is like trying to play golf during an earthquake.
Sylvester Stallone

One lesson you better learn if you want to be in politics is that you never go out on a golf course and beat the President.
Lyndon B. Johnson

There are two things that won't last long in this world, and that's dogs chasing cars and pros putting for pars.
Lee Trevino

I played golf. I did not get a hole in one, but I did hit a guy. That was way more satisfying.
Mitch Hedberg

No man has mastered golf until he realizes that his good shots are accidents and his bad shots are good exercise.
Eugene R. Black

One of the reasons Arnie Palmer is playing so well is that, before each final round, his wife takes out his balls and kisses them. Oh my God, what have I just said.
US Open TV Commentator

I was three over. One over a house, one over a patio, and one over a swimming pool.
George Brett

Splosh! One of the finest sights in the world: the other man's ball dropping in the water - preferably so that he can see it but cannot quite reach it and has therefore to leave it there, thus rendering himself so mad that he loses the next hole as well.
Henry Longhurst

If it wasn't for golf, I don't know what I'd be doing. If my IQ had been two points lower, I'd have been a plant somewhere.
Lee Trevino

I'll take the two-stroke penalty, but I'll be damned if I'll play it where it lays.
Elaine Johnson (after her ball ended up in her bra)

Fairway: a narrow strip of mown grass that separates two groups of golfers looking for lost balls in the rough.
Henry Beard

A ball you can see in the rough from 50 yards away is not yours.

Anon

Golfers who carry ball retrievers are gatherers, not hunters. Their dreams are no longer of conquest, but only of salvage.

David Owen

We have 51 golf courses in Palm Springs. He [President Ford] never decides which course he will play until after the first tee shot.

Bob Hope

It does look like a very good exercise. But what is the little white ball for?

US President Ulysses S. Grant

Alaska would be an ideal place for a golf course – mighty few trees and damn few ladies' foursomes.

Rex Lardner

I am playing like Tarzan and scoring like Jane.

Chi Chi Rodriguez

Playing Augusta is like playing a Salvador Dali landscape. I expected a clock to fall out of the trees and hit me in the face.

David Feherty

I played crap, he played crap. He just outcrapped me.

Wayne Grady

Some guys get so nervous playing for their own money, the greens don't need fertilizing for a year.
Dave Hill

I play golf every chance I get. The world needs more laughter.
Bob Hope

A trick shot is a 'Dennis Wise' – a 'nasty five-footer'.
Des Kelly

A lucky bounce is an OJ Simpson- 'got away with it somehow'.
Des Kelly

What do I have to shoot to win the tournament? The rest of the field.
Roger Maltbie

My career started slowly and then tapered off.
Gary McCord

Pebble Beach Golf Club is a 300-acre unplayable lie.
Jim Murray

A lot of guys who have never choked, have never been in the position to do so.
Tom Watson

He used to be fairly indecisive, but now he's not so certain
Peter Alliss

Carnoustie is like an ugly, old hag who speaks the truth no matter how painful. But it's only when you add up your score you hear exactly what she thinks of you.
Tom Watson

A golf course manager is the keeper of lawn order.
Erica H. Stux

Like all Saturday foursomes it is in difficulties. One of the patients is zigzagging about the fairway like a liner pursued by submarines.
P. G. Wodehouse

Two balls in the water. By God, I have got a good mind to jump in and make it four.
Simon Hobday

When you play the game for fun...it's fun. When you play it for a living...it's a game of sorrows.
Gary Player

Keep your eye on the club. Nothing is more embarrassing than throwing a club and asking your partner where it went.
Glen Waggoner

Muirfield without wind is like a lady undressed. No challenge.
Tom Watson

What changes would I like to see to golf? I would like to see the holes made bigger.
Fuzzy Zoeller

Victory is everything. You can spend the money, but you can never spend the memories.
Ken Venturi

What you have to understand is that three bad shots and one good shot still make par. You see golf is a game of recovery.
Bobby Jones

Men who would face torture without a word become blasphemous at the short fourteenth. It is clear that the game of golf may well be included in that category of intolerable provocations which may legally excuse or mitigate behavior not otherwise excusable.
AP Herbert

A golf match is a test of your skill against your opponents' luck.
Anon

Every time a golfer makes a birdie, he must subsequently make two triple bogeys to restore the fundamental equilibrium of the universe.
Anon

Everyone replaces his divot after a perfect approach shot.
Anon

Golf balls are like eggs. They're white. They're sold by the dozen. And you need to buy fresh ones each week.
Anon

Hazards attract; fairways repel.

Anon

The reason why the Road hole (17th) at St. Andrews is such a great par-4 is because it's a par-5.

Ben Crenshaw

THE OLDER GOLFER

Golf is a game that needlessly prolongs the lives of some of our most useless citizens.
Bob Hope

I went to play golf and tried to shoot my age, but I shot my weight instead.
Bob Hope

A game in which you claim the privileges of age, and retain the playthings of childhood.
Samuel Johnson

Golf balls are attracted to water as unerringly as the eye of a middle-aged man to a female bosom.
Michael Green

I'll shoot my age if I have to live to be 105.
Bob Hope

Any game where a man 60 can beat a man 30 ain't no game.
Burt Shotten

What's nice about our tour is you can't remember your bad shots.
Bob Bruce, about the senior tour

The older I get, the better I used to be.
Lee Trevino

The older you get the stronger the wind gets... and it's always in your face.
Jack Nicklaus

You know you're on the Senior Tour when your back goes out more than you do.
Bob Bruce

Years ago, we discovered the exact point, the dead center of middle age. It occurs when you are too young to take up golf and too old to rush up to the net.
Franklin P. Adams

One of the nice things about the Senior Tour is that we can take a cart and cooler. If your game is not going well, you can always have a picnic.
Lee Trevino

I still swing the way I used to, but when I look up the ball is going in a different direction.
Lee Trevino

Retire to what? I'm a golfer and a fisherman. I've got no place to retire to.
Julius Boros

Like a lot of fellows on the Senior Tour, I have a furniture problem. My chest has fallen into my drawers.
Billy Caspar

Some of these legends have been around golf a long time. When they mention a good grip, they are talking about their dentures.
Bob Hope

I told the Master's Chairman that I was getting too old to play, but he kept saying, 'Gene, they don't want to see you play; they just want to see if you are still alive'.
Gene Sarazen

I'm working as hard as I can to get my life and my cash to run out at the same time. If I can just die after lunch Tuesday, everything would be perfect.
Doug Sanders

I can't wait to be that age and hanging out with a bunch of people hanging out all day playing golf and going to the beach, all my own age. We'd be laughing and having a good time and getting loopy on our prescription drugs. Driving golf carts around. I can't wait.
Cameron Diaz

If there's a golf course in heaven, I hope it's like Augusta National. I just don't want an early tee time.
Gary Player

His nerves. His memory. And I can't remember the third thing.
Lee Trevino, recounting what goes as the golfer ages.

CADDIES

A caddie is someone who accompanies a golfer and didn't see the ball either.
Anon

If each time a player and caddie split up was actually a divorce, most Tour players would have been 'married' more times than Zsa Zsa and Liz combined.
Peter Jacobsen

Many a golfer prefers a golf cart to a caddy because the cart cannot count, criticize or laugh.
Anon

I never kick my ball in the rough or improve my lie in a sand trap. For that I have a caddy.
Bob Hope

The only useful putting advice I got from my caddy was to keep the ball low.
Chi Chi Rodriguez

Nobody bar you and your caddie care what you do out there, and if your caddie is betting against you, he doesn't care, either.
Lee Trevino

My game is so bad I gotta hire three caddies- one to walk the left rough, one for the right, and one for the middle. And the one in the middle doesn't have much to do.
Dave Hill

If I needed advice from my caddie, he'd be hitting the shots and I'd be carrying the bag.

Bobby Jones

If your caddie coaches you on the tee 'Hit it down the left side with a little draw', ignore him. All you do on the tee is try not to hit your caddie.

Jim Murray

TECHNIQUE

I was swinging like a toilet door on a prawn trawler.
David Feherty

If profanity had an influence on the flight of the ball, the game of golf would be played far better than it is.
Horace G. Hutchinson

Jim Furyk's swing looks like an octopus falling out of a tree.
David Feherty

My swing is so bad I look like a caveman killing his lunch.
Lee Trevino

If a lot of people gripped a knife and fork the way they do a golf club, they'd starve to death.
Sam Snead

The reason the pro tells you to keep your head down is so you can't see him laughing.
Phyllis Diller

They throw their clubs backwards, and that's wrong. You should always throw a club ahead of you so that you don't have to walk any extra distance to get it.
Tommy Bolt

I'm not saying my golf game went bad, but if I grew tomatoes, they'd come up sliced.
Miller Barber

It looks like a one-armed man trying to wrestle a snake in a phone booth.
David Feherty, on Jim Furyk's swing

Real golfers, no matter what the provocation, never strike a caddie with the driver. The sand wedge is far more effective.
Huxtable Pippey

My handicap? Woods and irons.
Chris Codiroli

If I can hit a curveball, why can't I hit a ball that is standing still on a course?
Larry Nelson

The fun you get from golf is in direct ratio to the effort you don't put into it.
Bob Allen

I once showed Pat Bradley my swing and said, 'What do I do next?' Pat replied, 'Wait till the pain dies down'.
Bob Hope

Actually, the only time I ever took out a one-iron was to kill a tarantula. And it took a seven to do that.
Jim Murray

I'm hitting the woods just great, but I'm having a terrible time getting out of them.
Harry Toscano

I can airmail the golf ball, but sometimes I don't put the right address on it.
Jim Dent

A golf ball is like a clock. Always hit it at 6 o'clock and make it go toward 12 o'clock. But make sure you're in the same time zone.
Chi Chi Rodriguez

Through years of experience I have found that air offers less resistance than dirt.
Jack Nicklaus

Golf is an awkward set of bodily contortions designed to produce a graceful result.
Tommy Armour

As far as swing and techniques are concerned, I don't know diddly squat. When I'm playing well, I don't even take aim.
Fred Couples

Art (Rosenbaum) said he wanted to get more distance. I told him to hit it and run backward.
Ken Venturi

His driving is unbelievable. I don't go that far on my holidays.
Ian Baker-Finch, on John Daly

Reverse every natural instinct and do the opposite of what you are inclined to do, and you will probably come very close to having a perfect golf swing.
Ben Hogan

That's a great shot with that swing.
David Feherty

The secret of missing a tree is to aim straight at it.
Michael Green

You can talk to a fade but a hook won't listen.
Lee Trevino

The golf swing is like a suitcase into which we are trying to pack one too many things.
John Updike

A golf swing is a collection of corrected mistakes.
Carol Mann

Watching Phil Mickelson play golf is like watching a drunk chasing a balloon near the edge of a cliff.
David Feherty

Colin Montgomerie has a face like a warthog that has been stung by a wasp.
David Feherty

The golf swing is like sex: you can't be thinking of the mechanics of the act while you're doing it.
Dave Hill

They say "practice" makes perfect " Of course, it doesn't. For the vast majority of golfers, it merely consolidates imperfection.
Henry Longhurst

Golf tips are like aspirin. One may do you good, but if you swallow the whole bottle, you will be lucky to survive.
Harvey Penick

The most exquisitely satisfying act in the world of golf is that of throwing a club. The full backswing, the delayed wrist action, the flowing follow through, followed by that unique whirring sound, reminiscent only of a passing flock of starlings, are without parallel in sport.
Henry Longhurst

I hate a hook. It nauseates me. I could vomit when I see one. It's like a rattlesnake in your pocket.
Lee Trevino

The worst club in my bag is my brain.
Chris Perry

Dividing the swing into its parts is like dissecting a cat. You'll have blood and guts and bones all over the place. But you won't have a cat.
Ernest Jones

My golf swing is a bit like ironing a shirt. You get one side smoothed out, turn it over and there is a big wrinkle on the other side. Then you iron that one out, turn it over and there is yet another wrinkle.
Tom Watson

The golf swing is among the most stressful and unnatural acts in sports, short of cheering for the Yankees.
Brad Faxon

When male golfers wriggle their feet to get their stance right, they look exactly like cats preparing to pee.
Jilly Cooper

When a pro hits it left to right it is called a fade. When an amateur hits it left to right it is called a slice.
Peter Jacobsen

Follow through: the part of the swing that takes place after the ball has been hit, but before the club has been thrown.
Henry Beard

I won't try to describe his game, beyond saying that the way he played, it would have taken three years of solid practice to work up to where he could be called a duffer.
Paul Gallico

My backswing off the first tee had put him in mind of an elderly lady of dubious morals trying to struggle out of a dress too tight around the shoulders.
Patrick Campbell

The difference between a good golf shot and a bad one is the same as the difference between a beautiful woman and a plain one - a matter of millimeters.
Ian Fleming

There are three ways of learning golf: by study, which is the most wearisome; by imitation, which is the most fallacious; and by experience, which is the most bitter.
Robert Browning

Hit it hard. It will land somewhere.
Mark Calcavecchia

You've just one problem. You stand too close to the ball after you've hit it.
Sam Snead

Golf is an awkward set of bodily contortions designed to produce a graceful result.
Tommy Armour

If your best golf shots are the practice swing and the "gimme putt", you might want to reconsider this game.
Anon

BUSINESS

If you break 100, watch your golf. If you break 80, watch your business.
Joey Adams

Born to golf. Forced to work.
Anon

The proper score for a businessman golfer is 90. If he is better than that he is neglecting his business. If he's worse, he's neglecting his golf.
St Andrews Rotary Club Member

Golf is my profession. Show business is just to pay the green fees.
Bob Hope

There are two basic rules which should never be broken. Be subtle. And don't, for God's sake, try to do business with anyone who's having a bad game.
William Davis

PSYCHOLOGY

I'd play every day if I could. It's cheaper than a shrink and there are no telephones on my golf cart.
Brent Musburger

Golf is an open exhibition of overweening ambition, courage deflated by stupidity, skill scoured by a whiff of arrogance.
Alistair Cooke

One thing about golf is you don't know why you play bad and why you play good.
George Archer

My body is here, but my mind has already teed off .
Anon

I've heard people say putting is 50 percent technique and 50 percent mental. I really believe it is 50 percent technique and 90 percent positive thinking, see, but that adds up to 140 percent, which is why nobody is 100 percent sure how to putt.
Chi Chi Rodriguez

A leading difficulty with the average player is that he totally misunderstands what is meant by concentration. He may think he is concentrating hard when he is merely worrying.
Bobby Jones

Golf is the loneliest of games, not excluding postal chess.
Peter Dobereiner

Colin Montgomery is a few French fries short of a Happy Meal.
David Feherty

My psychiatrist prescribed a game of golf as an antidote to the feelings of euphoria I experience from time to time.
Bruce Lansky

Some golfers lie awake at night, and brood on what went wrong; I'd rather think of what went right. It doesn't take as long.
Dick Emmons

Let's face it, 95 percent of this game is mental. A guy plays lousy golf, he doesn't need a pro, he needs a shrink.
Tom Murphy

Golf is good for the soul. You get so mad at yourself you forget to hate your enemies.
Will Rogers

Since bad shots come in groups of three, a fourth bad shot is actually the beginning of the next group of three.
Anon

Any change works for a maximum of 3 holes and a minimum of not at all
Anon

The Equipment

The trouble that most of us find with the modern matched sets of clubs is that they don't really seem to know any more about the game than the old ones did.
Robert Browning

Golf is an ineffectual attempt to put an elusive ball into an obscure hole with implements ill-adapted to the purpose.
Woodrow Wilson

My clubs are well used, but unfortunately not used well.
Jack Burrell

The other day I broke 70. That's a lot of clubs.
Henry Youngman

I get upset over a bad shot just like anyone else. But it's silly to let the game get to you. When I miss a shot I just think what a beautiful day it is. And what pure fresh air I'm breathing. Then I take a deep breath. I have to do that. That's what gives me the strength to break the club.
Bob Hope

The ball retriever is not long enough to get my putter out of the tree.
Brian Weis

If you are going to throw a golf club, it is important to throw it ahead of you, down the fairway, so you don't waste energy going back to pick it up.
Tommy Bolt

Golf balls are like eggs. they're white. They're sold by the dozen and a week later you have to buy more.

Anon

Golfing Glossary

An Adolf: *Taking two shots in a bunker.*

Circus Tent: *A big top*

An Arthur Scargill: *Great strike but a poor result.*

A Condom: *Safe but didn't feel right.*

An Elephant's bottom: *It's high and it stinks.*

John Wayne Bobbitt: *A vicious slice, ended up short*

A Gerry Adams: *A provisional*

Kate Moss: *Very thin, but it worked*

A Dennis Wise: *Nasty little five-footer.*

A Danny de Vito: *A laughable five-footer*

A Diego Maradona: *A very nasty five-footer*

Ladyboy: *Looks easy, but more to it than meets the eye*

A Rock Hudson: *Thought it was straight, but it wasn't.*

Mick Jagger: *A big lip out*

A Cuban: *Needs one more revolution.*

A Brazilian: *Hits the narrow strip down the middle.*

An Anna Kournikova: *Looks great, but unlikely to get a result.*

A Vinnie Jones: *Nasty kick when you're not expecting it.*

A Bill Clinton: *a bad lie*

Best mate's wife: *out of bounds*

A Liberace: *playing down a different hole*

Baghdad: *GUR*

A Bin Laden: *In the water and never to be found again.*

A Tony Blair: *Too much spin.*

A James Joyce: *An impossible read*

A Colonel Gaddafi: *Dangerous in sand*

An Edward Kennedy: *Erratic drive straight into the water*

A Yasser Arafat: *Ugly and in the sand.*

A Nancy Pelosi: *Way to the left and out of bounds.*

An oxymoron: *An easy par-3*

A Tiger Woods: *Wrong Hole.*

THE GOLFER AND HIS CADDIE

Golfer: You've got to be the worst caddy in the world.
Caddie: I don't think so. That would just be too much of a coincidence.

Caddie: Are you a scratch player?
Golfer: I sure am - every time I hit the ball I scratch my head and wonder where it went.

Golfer: Well, I have never played this badly before.
Caddie: I didn't realize you had played before, Sir

Player: Can we get there with a 5 iron?
Caddie: Eventually.

Golfer: Notice any improvement today, Jimmy?
Caddie: Yes, ma'am. You've had your hair done.

Golfer: I'm going to drown myself in the lake.
Caddie: Think you can keep your head down that long?

Golf: This golf is a funny game.
Caddie: It's not supposed to be.

Player: What should I hit?
Caddie: Try the fairway.

Golfer: This is the worst course I've ever played on.
Caddie: This isn't the golf course. We left that an hour ago.

Golfer: What's the problem with my golf game?
Caddie: You're standing too close to the ball ... after you've hit it.

Golfer: I'd move heaven and earth to break 100 on this course.
Caddie: Try heaven. You've already moved most of the earth.

Golfer: Please stop checking your watch all the time. It's very distracting.
Caddie: It's not a watch – it's a compass.

Golfer: I want a caddie who can count and keep the score. What's 3 and 4 and 5 add up to?
Caddie: 11 sir.
Golfer: Good, you'll do perfectly.

Golfer: How do you like my game?
Caddie: Oh, it's a great game, but personally I prefer golf.

Golfer: I'm ready to go for this par-5 green in two, but there's still a group on the green. What should I do?
Caddie: Well, you have two options: you can go ahead and shank it right now, or wait for the green to clear and then top the ball half way there.

Golf: What's the easiest shot in golf?
Caddie. Your fourth putt.

Golfer: Do you think it's a sin to play on Sunday?
Caddy: The way you play, it's a sin on any day.

Golfer: Do you think my game is improving?
Caddy: Yes, you miss the ball much closer now.

Golfer: Hey caddie, would you wade into that pond and see if you can find my ball?
Caddie: Why?
Golfer: It's my lucky ball.

Golfer: That can't be my ball, it's too old.
Caddy: It's been a long time since we teed off, sir.

Made in the USA
Middletown, DE
22 December 2017